START-UP

# SCIENCE

# ELECTRICITY

Claire Llewellyn

Published by Evans Brothers Limited
2A Portman Mansions
Chiltern Street
London W1U 6NR



Produced for Evans Brothers Limited by
White-Thomson Publishing Ltd.
2/3 St Andrew's Place
Lewes, East Sussex BN7 1UP

**Printed in China by WKT Company Limited**

Editor: Dereen Taylor
Consultants: Les Jones, Science Consultant, Manchester Education Partnership; Norah Granger, former primary headteacher and senior lecturer in education, University of Brighton
Designer: Leishman Design

*Cover:* All photographs by Chris Fairclough



British Library Cataloguing in Publication Data
Llewellyn, Claire
Electricity - (Start-up science)
1.Electricity - Juvenile literature
I.Title
537

ISBN: 0 237 52592 5

**Acknowledgements:**
Special thanks to the following for their help and involvement in the preparation of this book: Staff and pupils at Elm Grove Primary School, Brighton, Liz Price and family and friends.

**Picture Acknowledgements:**
Liz Price 20, 21.
Mary Evans Picture Library 9.
All other photographs by Chris Fairclough.

# Contents

# Electricity in school

**It's a busy day at school. Everyone has machines to help them do their work. These machines all run on electricity.**

**Jane is working at the computer.**

**The head teacher is talking on the telephone.**



**machines electricity computer**

**Ernest is doing sums using his calculator.**

**The cook is taking food out of the freezer.**

**telephone   calculator   freezer**

# Electrical appliances

**Many things run on electricity.**
**They are called electrical appliances.**

**▼ Look at the things in this picture.**

**Which of them are electrical appliances?**
**Which of them are not?**

George made a list of the electrical appliances in school. He went into a classroom, the office, the kitchen and the hall.

| Classroom | Office | Kitchen | Hall |
|---|---|---|---|
| lights | lights | lights | lights |
| computer | computer | fridge | heater |
| printer | telephone | freezer | |
| tape recorder | printer | kettle | |
| clock | fax machine | mixer | |
| | photocopier | | |
| | clock | | |
| | calculator | | |

Which room has the most appliances?
Make a list of the appliances in your kitchen at home.

photocopier mixer heater

# What does it do?

**Some electrical appliances give out light, like a torch. Some give out heat, like a fire. Some make sounds, like a tape recorder. Some have moving parts, like a washing machine.**

**▶ Match each of these electrical appliances with the words below.**

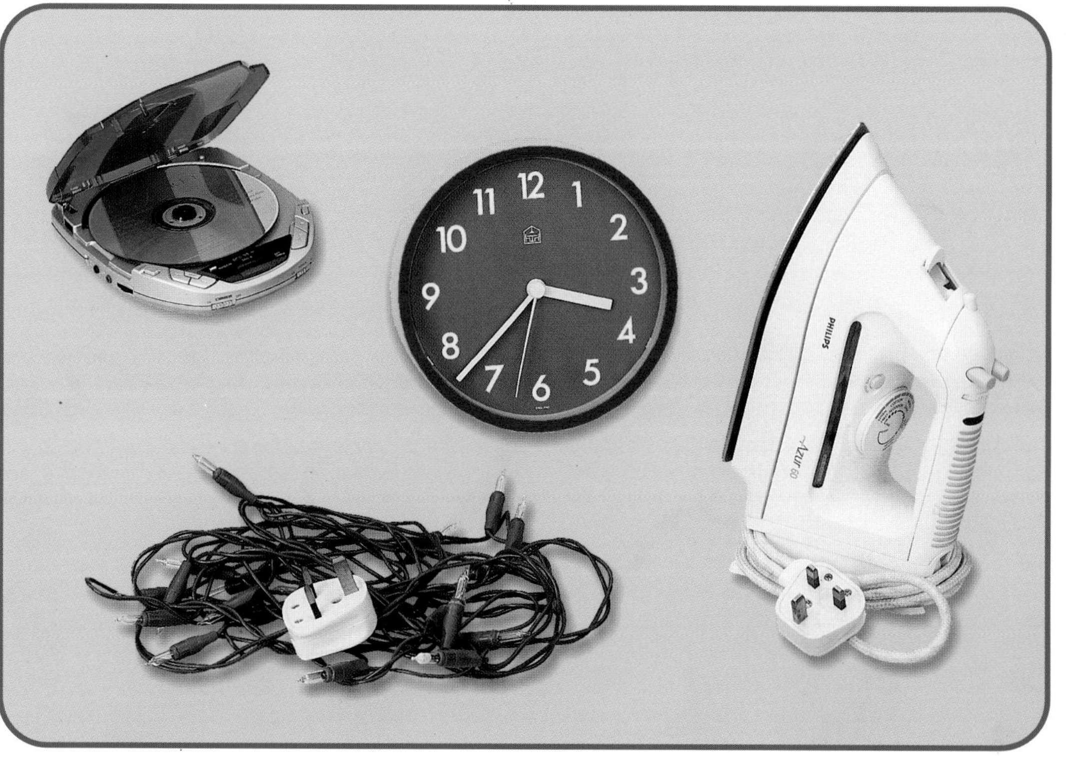

light heat sound moving parts

**light heat sounds**

In the past, before there was electricity, people used different kinds of appliances in their homes.

How did people light their homes?

▶ This is how people made toast, one hundred years ago.

moving parts different

# Mains electricity

◀ Jake's dad is cleaning the carpet. He plugs the vacuum cleaner into a socket in the wall. Then he switches it on.

▲ When we plug electrical appliances into a socket, they use electricity from the mains. Electricity flows along the flex and into the machine.



socket switches on plug

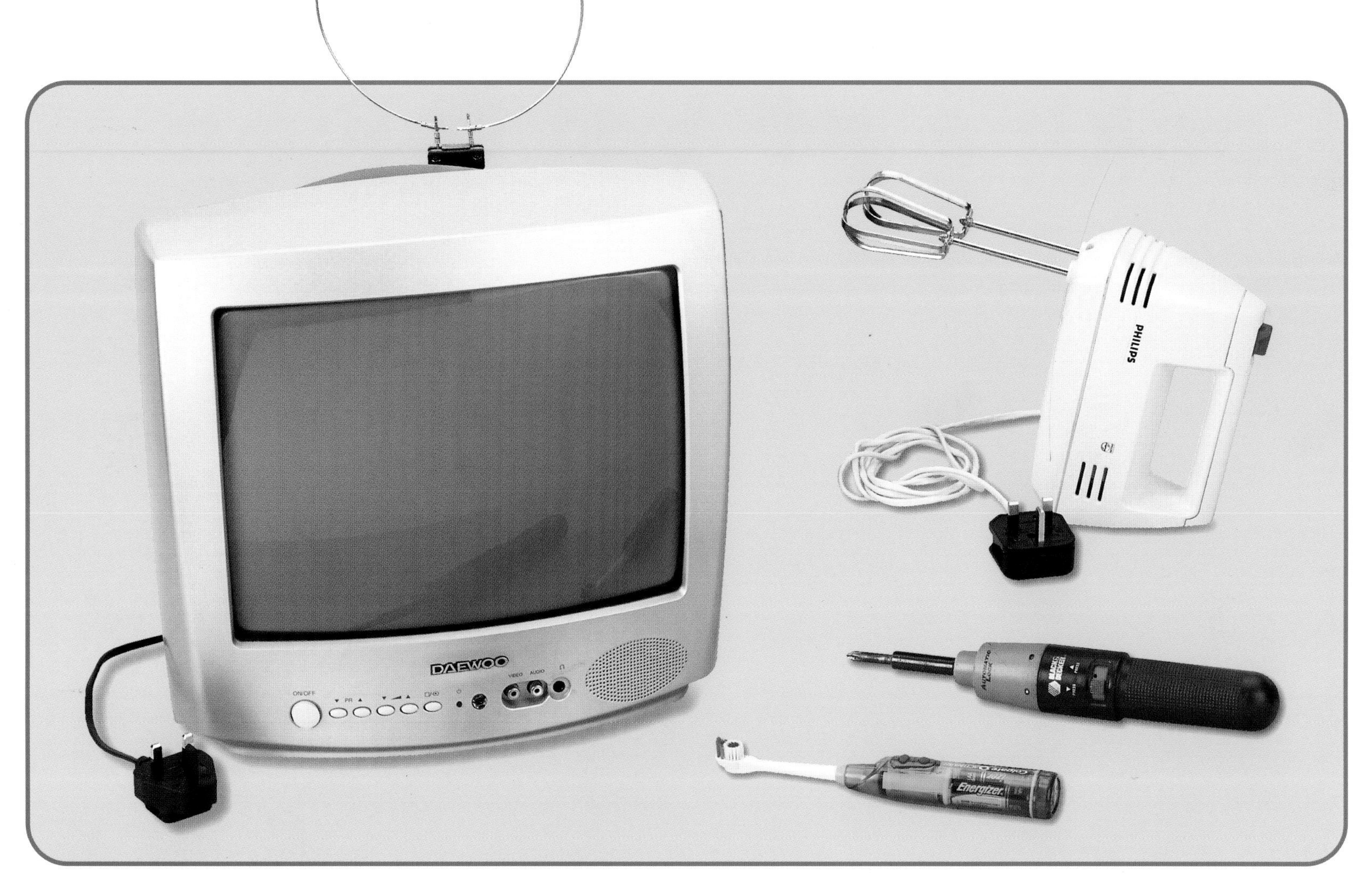


## WARNING!

**Never play with mains electricity. It can be very dangerous and can even kill us.**

**▲ Look at these appliances. Which ones use electricity from the mains? How can you tell?**

mains flows flex dangerous

# Looking at batteries

Alex's remote control car does not run on mains electricity. It runs on batteries instead. Batteries store electricity.

◀ The remote control handset also runs on batteries. Alex needs to fit a new battery. Can you see the right way to put it in?



batteries   store

Small batteries store a little electricity. Big batteries store much more. Look at the objects in the pictures.

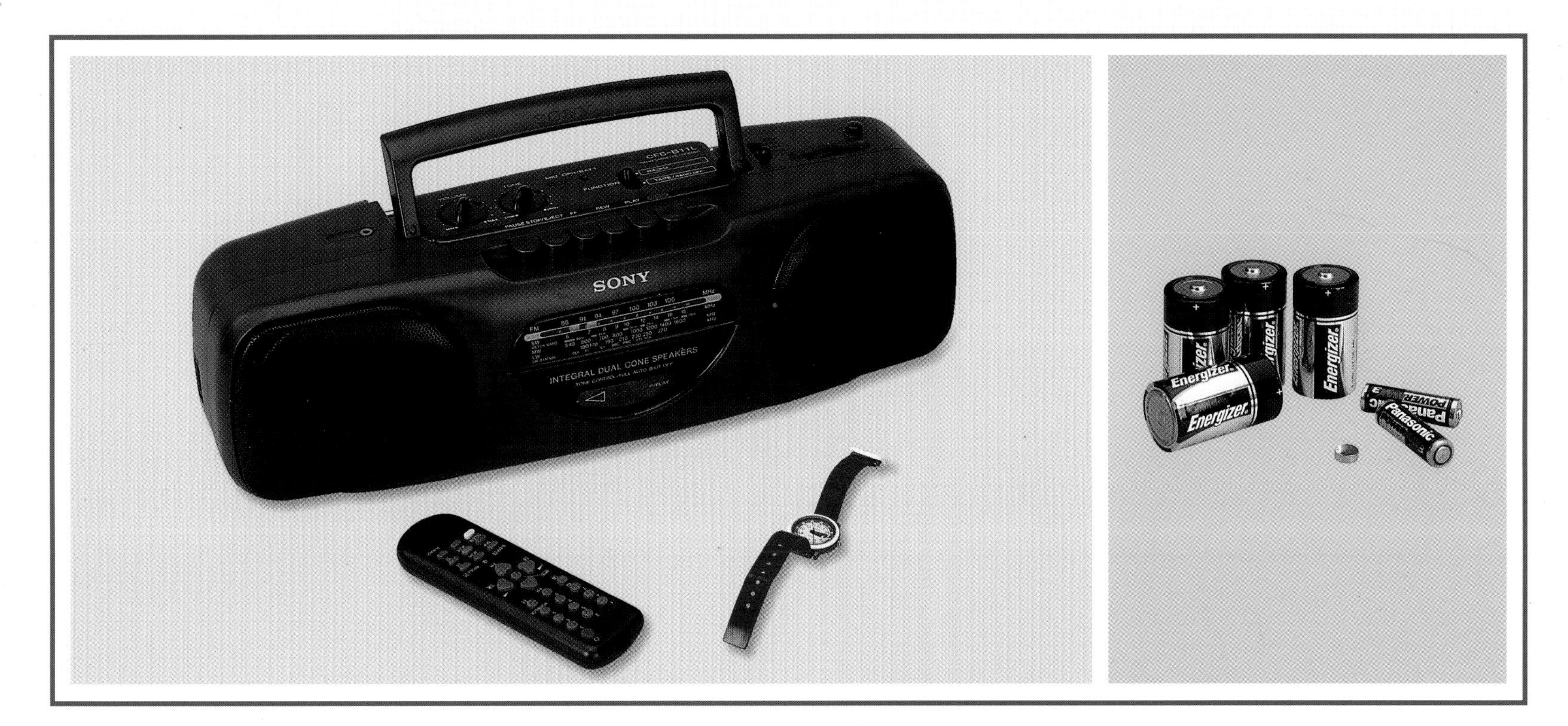


Can you match each appliance to the right batteries?
What other things use batteries?

**WARNING!**
Batteries contain poisons and should not be put near your mouth.

poisons

# Lights and light bulbs

▶ When Olivia's mum switches on the lamp, the light bulb lights up.

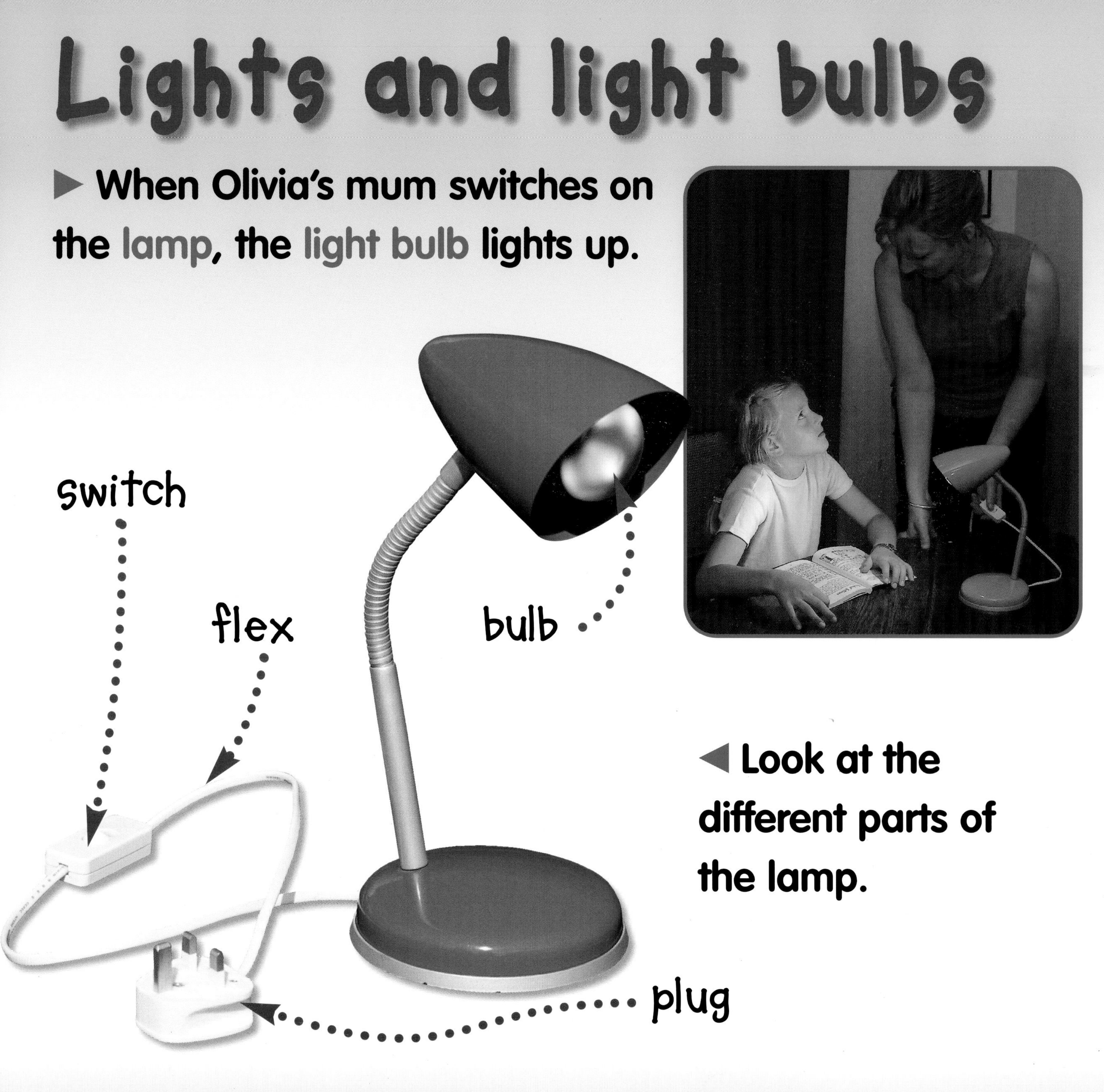


◀ Look at the different parts of the lamp.



lamp light bulb

Look closely at another light bulb. Inside, you can see a metal wire called a filament. This is the part that shines brightly when you switch the light on.

filament

# WARNING!

Never touch electrical switches or plugs when you have wet hands. Water and electricity together are very dangerous.

metal wire filament water

# Light up a bulb

**Owen is going to make his own light. His teacher has given him everything he needs.**

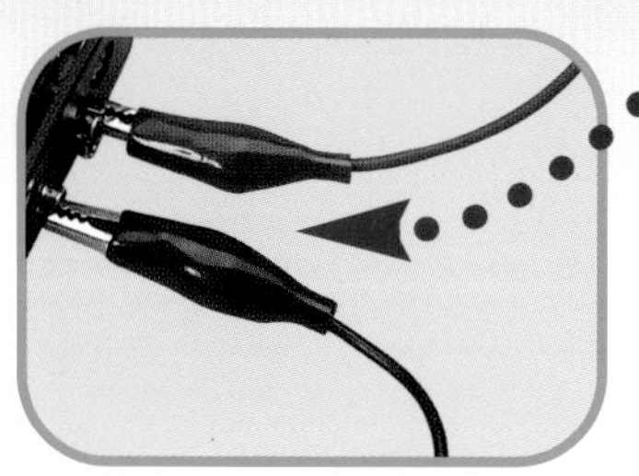

crocodile clips and plastic-coated wire

bulb

batteries

**To get electricity from the battery to the bulb, Owen needs to give it a pathway. This pathway is called a circuit.**

**► First Owen screws the bulb into the bulb holder.**

**pathway circuit bulb holder**

▼ Then he **connects** the wires to the batteries using the **crocodile clips**.

▼ Finally he connects the wires to the bulb holder.

Hooray! The bulb lights up!

**connects  crocodile clips**

# What went wrong?

Harry and Mary cannot make their bulbs light up. There is a problem with their circuits.

▼ Can you see how Harry can fix his circuit?

▼ **There is a different problem with Mary's circuit. Can you see what it is?**

# How a circuit works

▼ **These children are acting out the circuit to show how it works. When the children hold hands D's bulb lights up.**

**This shows how electricity flows around a circuit.**

▼ **When two children drop hands, D's bulb goes out.**

**Electricity cannot flow because the circuit is broken.**

**A = battery B and C = crocodile clips and plastic-coated wire D = bulb holder with bulb**

**broken**

# Further information for

## New words listed in the text:

batteries
broken
bulb holder
calculator
circuit
computer
connects
crocodile clips
dangerous
different
electrical appliances
electricity
filament
flex
flows
freezer
heat
heater
lamp
light
lights
light bulb
machines
mains
metal wire
mixer
moving parts
on
pathway
photocopier
plug
poisons
printer
socket
sounds
store
switches
telephone
water

## Possible Activities

### PAGES 4-5

Ask the children to list three ways in which they use electricity.

Can the children guess how many electrical appliances they have in their homes? Is it 0-10; 10-20 or 20+? Ask them to count the appliances when they go home. Were they right?

### PAGES 6-7

Find a big picture of a typical kitchen. Ask the children to identify all the electric machines. Can they think what people used in the past before they used electricity?

List all the electrical appliances in the classroom.

### PAGES 8-9

Many electrical appliances do more than one thing. Can the children think of machines that produce light and sound (e.g. electric doorbell) or movement and sound (e.g. CD-player), etc.

In the past there was no electricity. Which electrical appliance would the children miss most?

### PAGES 10-11

Discuss the dangers associated with electricity. Tell the children that electricity can kill, and that they must never play with plugs, sockets or wires or go near cables or pylons. Explain the danger of broken plugs and frayed wires. Tell the children about the dangers of water and electricity.

Discuss why we use pull cords in bathrooms to switch on lights, showers and fans.

### PAGES 12-13

Make a list of all the appliances in the classroom that use batteries. Make a collection of batteries and list what each one can be used for.

Allow children to remove the batteries from simple devices such as torches and remote controls. Can they put them back the right way?

# Parents and Teachers

### PAGES 14-15

Make a collection of light bulbs (e.g. for fairy lights, torches, spotlights, etc.) Can the children see a filament in all of them?

Cut up a piece of electrical flex so that children can see the wires inside. Discuss how the plastic casing keeps the electricity 'locked' inside.

### PAGES 16-17

Allow the children to make circuits, using a buzzer instead of a bulb. Can they make the buzzer work?

Ask the children to draw a working circuit and label the different parts.

### PAGES 18-19

Make the well-known game in which a metal loop has to travel along a curved wire without touching it. If you touch the wire with the loop, you complete the circuit and the buzzer goes off. You will need a wooden base, two screws, a bent wire coat hanger, three wires, a buzzer and a battery.

Draw some circuits. Can the children predict which ones will and won't work? Ask them to test their ideas by making the circuits.

### PAGES 20-21

Make a list of electrical appliances that have an on/off switch. Do all the switches look the same?

Add a simple switch to an electric circuit by using a paper clip to make and break the contact between two drawing pins connected to the wires and pushed into a small piece of wood.

## Further Information

### BOOKS FOR CHILDREN

*Electricity* by Peter Riley
(Franklin Watts, 2003)

*Pocket Science: Where does electricity come from?*
by Susan Mayes
(Usborne, 2001)

*Toybox Science: Electricity*
by Chris Ollerenshaw and Pat Triggs
(A & C Black, 1999)

*Which Switch is Which?* by Sam Godwin
(Hodder Wayland, 2002)

*Why Does a Battery Make it Go?* by Jackie Holderness
(Franklin Watts, 2002)

### WEBSITES

www.howstuffworks.com

www.primaryresources.co.uk/science

# Index